THE 10™

Most Shocking Sports Scandals

Glen Downey

Series Editor
Jeffrey D. Wilhelm

Much thought, debate, and research went into choosing and ranking the 10 items in each book in this series. We realize that everyone has his or her own opinion of what is most significant, revolutionary, amazing, deadly, and so on. As you read, you may agree with our choices, or you may be surprised — and that's the way it should be!

an imprint of

■SCHOLASTIC

www.scholastic.com/librarypublishing

A Rubicon book published in association with Scholastic Inc.

Ru'bĭcon © 2008 Rubicon Publishing Inc.
www.rubiconpublishing.com

 is a trademark of The 10 Books

Associate Publisher: Kim Koh
Project Editor: Amy Land
Editorial Assistant: Nikki Yeh
Creative Director: Jennifer Drew
Project Manager/Designer: Jeanette MacLean
Graphic Designers: Doug Baines, Waseem Bashar, Brandon Köpke

The publisher gratefully acknowledges the following for permission to reprint copyrighted material in this book.

Every reasonable effort has been made to trace the owners of copyrighted material and to make due acknowledgment. Any errors or omissions drawn to our attention will be gladly rectified in future editions.

"Ruiz found out she can't run from the truth" (excerpt) by Bruce Lowitt, September 24, 1999. Copyright *St. Petersburg Times* 1999.

"Gold for Salé and Pelletier stirs world reaction" (excerpt) by CBC News, February 16, 2002. Permission courtesy of CBC.ca.

"Scandal hits Italian League" (excerpt) by Frank Dell'Apa. *The Boston Globe*, May 23, 2006. Reprinted with permission.

"Director John Sayles takes his run at plate" (excerpt) by Bruce Blackadar, *Toronto Star*, August 31, 1988. Reprinted with permission — Torstar Syndication Services.

Cover: Pete Rose–© Michael Williams/ZUMA/Corbis

Library and Archives Canada Cataloguing in Publication

Downey, Glen R., 1969-
    The 10 most shocking sports scandals / Glen Downey.

Includes index.
ISBN 978-1-55448-505-5

    1. Readers (Elementary). 2. Readers—Sports—Corrupt practices. I. Title. II. Title: Ten most shocking sports scandals.

PE1117.D69374 2007a   428.6   C2007-906704-2

1 2 3 4 5 6 7 8 9 10   10   17 16 15 14 13 12 11 10 09 08

Printed in Singapore

Contents

10

18

38

THE SHOCKING TRUTH

Imagine the pressure of being a top athlete. Everything depends on how fast you run, how hard you hit, and how many fans you draw to the stadium. The ability to break records — by mere fractions of a second — can lead to big-time bonuses. These athletes devote their lives to being the best. So why on earth do some of them become involved in scandals that put their careers, and even their lives, at risk? There's no easy answer, but we do know that almost everyone loves to read these stories of shame.

The 10 Most Shocking Sports Scandals presents the worst of the worst. These are the scandals that live on in infamy. They were so outrageous that they overshadowed the accomplishments of those who deserved to be recognized for their achievements.

When ranking these scandals, we considered the following criteria: the scandal had to attract the fascination and outrage of sports fans and the public. The scandal had to have a significant impact on the sport concerned; and it had to have serious consequences for the people involved.

infamy: *famous disgrace*

WHICH IS THE MOST SHOCKING SPORTS SCANDAL?

Police officers protect Rosie Ruiz from fans after the 1980 Boston Marathon.

1980 BOSTON MARATHON
W50
TIGER SHOES

AL RUN

ROSIE RUIZ—© BETTMANN/CORBIS

MAJOR PLAYERS: Rosie Ruiz and Jacqueline Gareau

SHOCK FACTOR: Ruiz didn't run a whole marathon — yet she was declared the winner.

In October 1979, Rosie Ruiz ran the New York City Marathon in two hours, 56 minutes, and 29 seconds. It was her very first marathon. This allowed her to qualify for the Boston Marathon in 1980.

The Boston Marathon is an annual long-distance event that is open to male and female athletes. In this marathon, competitors must run 26 miles. In 1980, professional runners, including Jacqueline Gareau, were up for the challenge. When Ruiz, an unknown athlete, became the female winner, all the runners and spectators were shocked. Something wasn't right about Ruiz's win: she didn't look tired or sweaty! After studying tapes and photos, and conducting interviews, marathon officials learned that Ruiz started running the race close to the finish line.

Officials asked Ruiz to return her medal, but she refused! She insisted that she had run the whole race. Turn the page to discover the consequences Ruiz had to face in this #10 scandal.

RUIZ'S UNREAL RUN

BEFORE THE STORM

Ruiz had some stiff competition in the 1980 Boston Marathon. She was running in the same race as Jacqueline Gareau and former Boston Marathon winner Bill Rodgers. The Boston Marathon has separate categories for men and women — Rodgers won in the men's category. When Gareau completed the race, she found Ruiz on a podium accepting the female winner's wreath.

During a press conference, Ruiz shows a certificate of her participation in the 1979 New York Marathon. She was trying to strengthen her case that she was the winner of the 1980 Boston Marathon. Instead, it was discovered that she had cheated in both races!

A SCANDALOUS AFFAIR

After interviews and photo and video examinations, the truth was revealed: Ruiz had not run the entire race. Rather, she had joined the race a few miles away from the finish line. Ruiz wouldn't admit she was wrong, even when there was evidence of her cheating. She said, "I don't have to prove myself innocent … I know I ran it." Another truth erupted during the scandal: Ruiz had also cheated in the New York City Marathon by taking the subway! The actual winner of the 1979 New York Marathon was Grete Waitz, who clocked in at 2:27:33.

THE AFTERMATH

Ruiz's winning title at the Boston Marathon was taken away from her, and she was banned from participating in future marathons. Gareau was crowned the female winner of the 1980 Boston Marathon. Ruiz was fired from her job soon after the Boston Marathon scandal. Ever since Ruiz's dishonest act, marathon runners must attach computer chips on their shoelaces. These chips keep track of when runners start and finish the races.

Quick Fact

In a 2005 interview, Jacqueline Gareau, the actual winner of the 1980 Boston Marathon, told the *Montreal Gazette* that she felt sorry for Ruiz. "I just feel sad for her in some way. This is not a great life, to [cheat] like that."

10

Ruiz found out she can't run from the truth

A **newspaper article** from *St. Petersburg Times*
By Bruce Lowitt, September 24, 1999

Who are you?

It was a legitimate question posed by Bill Rodgers, who had just won his fourth Boston Marathon. The woman beside him … was Rosie Ruiz, who had just won her first …

When she crossed the finish line on April 21, 1980, the clock read 2 hours, 31 minutes, 56 seconds, the third-fastest marathon ever by a woman and a record by a woman in this race. …

"I thought I was one of a few women to cross the finish line, until someone pulled me over and put this wreath on my head," Ruiz said. … "I think this is all a dream."

Try nightmare. …

There was no strong evidence that [Ruiz] had — or had not — run because the leading women were not recorded at the race's six checkpoints. …

Eight days and 10,000 photographs later, race officials ruled that Ruiz had not run the race. They could find no one who remembered seeing her through most of it. Jacqueline Gareau of Montreal, [Canada,] timed in 2:34:28, had led for the final 10 miles, they said. She was declared the winner. …

Asked if there would be any legal action against Ruiz, [race director Will Cloney] said: "I would rather hear that Jacqueline is the winner and let Rosie fade into the background."

… Rosie Ruiz — banned from the major marathons — became a synonym for cheating.

---

checkpoints: *locations where runners are timed*

ROSIE RUIZ–© BETTMANN/CORBIS; ALL OTHER IMAGES–SHUTTERSTOCK,ISTOCKPHOTO

The Expert Says…

" … Ruiz remains perhaps the most brazen cheater in U.S. history. And Gareau is the forgotten victim. "

— Jimmy Golen, Associated Press (AP) sportswriter

brazen: *shameless*

? Gareau is mentioned throughout this chapter, but the expert has called Gareau a "forgotten victim." Why do you think the expert chose to call Gareau this? Explain.

? Why do you think the author of the newspaper article chose to call Ruiz a "synonym for cheating"? If you don't know what a synonym is, find out.

Take Note

Ruiz's run is #10 because of its impact on long-distance running. Ruiz's shameless cheating encouraged marathon officials to keep track of runners more closely. Plus, the scandal had major consequences — Ruiz's first-place title was taken away from her!
• How would you describe Ruiz if you were to write about her for a magazine or newspaper?

5   4   3   2   1

The Spanish Paralympic basketball team celebrate their gold medal win at the 2000 Summer Paralympics.

TITY

MAJOR PLAYERS: Members of the Spanish Paralympic basketball team

SHOCK FACTOR: The Spanish Paralympic basketball team won a gold medal at the 2000 Summer Paralympics — but 10 of the players were not qualified to be on the team!

The Paralympic Games is a sports competition held after the Summer Olympics. It is for athletes with physical disabilities, such as those in wheelchairs. In 1996, the Paralympics began including intellectually disabled athletes. According to the Paralympics, an athlete is intellectually disabled if he or she has an IQ of 70 or less, as well as has "limitations" in life skills.

In 2000, the Summer Paralympic Games took place in Sydney, Australia. This was the first year that basketball for the intellectually disabled was introduced. Plus, this year would also be Spain's most successful participation in the Paralympics. Spain earned 107 medals — 37 of those were gold!

A month after Spain's incredible victories, a scandal exploded. In an issue of *Capital* magazine, Spanish journalist Carlos Ribagorda wrote a shocking article. He claimed that some of the players on Spain's Paralympic basketball team were not intellectually disabled. He knew this because he had faked intellectual disability to be on the team in order to expose their cheating. Fernando Martin Vicente, vice-president of the Spanish Paralympic Committee, claimed that intellectually disabled athletes actually had their IQs tested. But Ribagorda begged to differ …

IQ: *number expressing someone's score on an intelligence test (most results fall between 55 and 145)*

SECRET IDENTITY

BEFORE THE STORM

Anyone watching the Paralympic men's basketball finals knew that they were seeing something special. Russia had a good team, but the Spanish were unbelievable. Every time Spanish starters were on the floor, they dominated their opponents. The Russians lost by 24 points, and the Spanish basketball team took home the gold.

A SCANDALOUS AFFAIR

Journalist Carlos Ribagorda revealed that 10 basketball players on the Spanish team did not have intellectual disabilities. Ribagorda was on the team for two years, and not once was his IQ tested. Only two of the basketball players suffered from disabilities. Ribagorda also claimed that 15 athletes who were part of the whole Spanish Paralympic team, from table tennis to swimming, were not physically or intellectually disabled.

THE AFTERMATH

All of the Spanish Paralympic athletes had to return their medals. Even though he denied taking part in the scandal, Fernando Martin Vicente resigned from his position as vice-president of the Spanish Paralympic Committee. Since the scandal, intellectually disabled athletes have not been allowed to participate in the Paralympic Games. The International Paralympic Committee wants to look for ways to prevent cheating before it brings athletes with intellectual disabilities back into competition.

? Do you think it is right to ban all intellectually disabled athletes from the Paralympic Games? Explain why.

The Paralympic Games are now only open to athletes with physical disabilities.

Quick Fact
The Paralympics began in 1960 in Rome, Italy. Four hundred athletes and 23 countries participated in that year.

The Expert Says...

"It's a bizarre sign of how important success at the Paralympics has become, but it needs to be taken extremely seriously. Like drug-taking in mainstream [sports], there needs to be severe penalties ...

— Tanni Grey-Thompson, Paralympian wheelchair athlete

Paralympic Bombshells

The Spanish Paralympic Basketball team scandal was not the only shocker in the Paralympics. Check out these reports of other Paralympic scandals.

In 2004, Canadian Earle Connor, a 25-year-old sprinter with an amputated leg, tested positive for performance-enhancing drugs. Connor is considered to be one of the top Paralympic athletes in the world. The results of his drug test were revealed before he was scheduled to carry the Canadian flag at the opening ceremony of the 2004 Summer Paralympics in Athens, Greece. Connor was banned from participating in the Paralympics for two years.

performance-enhancing: *something that helps improve athletic performance*

According to *Sports Illustrated*, newspapers in Australia, England, and Canada reported that some wheelchair Paralympians have found ways to enhance their performance. Before competitions, they will stick themselves with pins. This increases their blood pressure by activating "fight or flight" responses. This type of behavior is considered cheating, and athletes who boost their blood pressure receive the same punishment as those caught with drugs.

Take Note

Like the 1980 Boston Marathon, the Spanish Paralympic basketball team cheated in a major competition. However, the Paralympic scandal is ranked #9 because it involved more than one athlete and caused intellectually disabled athletes to be suspended from the Paralympic Games.
- Compare the Paralympic controversies on this page with the Spanish Paralympic basketball team scandal. Which one of these sports scandals do you think is most shocking? Explain your answer.

5   4   3   2   1

The Salt Lake City Organizing Committee was headed by Dave Johnson (left) and Tom Welch. After they failed to win the 1998 Winter Games for Salt Lake City, they decided to do whatever it took to host the 2002 Winter Games in their city.

OCKER

MAJOR PLAYERS: International Olympic Committee (IOC) members and the Salt Lake City Organizing Committee (SLOC)

SHOCK FACTOR: The IOC members were bribed with cash, trips, and scholarships to favor Salt Lake City as the site of the 2002 Winter Olympics.

What a reason to celebrate! In 1995, the International Olympic Committee voted for Salt Lake City, Utah, to host the 2002 Winter Olympics. Salt Lake City received 54 out of 89 votes from IOC members, beating out competing cities for the bid. Residents of Salt Lake City were very excited. This meant that their city would be the focus of more than two billion people watching the televised Olympics!

Three years later, Salt Lake City made front-page news around the world. The Salt Lake Organizing Committee was being accused of bribing IOC members for their votes. As a rule, IOC officials are not allowed to accept gifts worth more than $150 from cities that are bidding to host the Olympics. But the value of the SLOC's bribes added up to a much larger amount. Cash, college scholarships, home and car repairs, vacations to Disney World, and tickets to the Super Bowl were just a few of the bribes IOC officials accepted. Leading the scandal were Tom Welch and Dave Johnson, the top officials of the SLOC.

OLYMPIC SHOCKER

BEFORE THE STORM

Salt Lake City failed in numerous attempts to win the bid to host the Winter Olympics. After it lost to Nagano, Japan, for the 1998 Games, the SLOC decided to try their hardest for the 2002 Games. In 1995, Salt Lake City announced that it was going to host the 2002 Winter Olympic Games!

A SCANDALOUS AFFAIR

Marc Hodler, a senior official of the IOC, revealed in 1998 that the Salt Lake City Organizing Committee cheated. Investigators from four different organizations looked into the claims, and evidence started coming to the surface. Welch and Johnson had spent millions of dollars on bribes and favors.

THE AFTERMATH

In 1999, 10 members quit the IOC on their own or were expelled for accepting bribes. Welch and Johnson were taken to court for fraud and bribery. Both were acquitted of criminal charges in 2003 because there was not enough evidence against them. The SLOC appointed a new leader and did a good job of staging the Olympic event. The scandal led to changes in the IOC, one of which forbids members to accept gifts from bidding cities.

acquitted: *declared not guilty*

? Do you think the IOC should impose stricter rules on its officials? Explain why.

Deedee Corradini (left) with Frank Joklik

The Expert Says...

" ... [the scandal marked] a watershed in the worst scandal in Olympic history and the start of a reform process to restore the luster of the five rings. "

— Duncan Mackay, reporter for the *Guardian Unlimited* newspaper

watershed: *turning point*
luster: *appearance*

Quick Fact

Deedee Corradini, 2002 Salt Lake City mayor, decided against seeking re-election after being linked to the scandal. Frank Joklik, former president of the SLOC, stepped down from his position after acknowledging bribery had taken place.

? Why do you think Salt Lake City Organizing Committee members wanted their city to host the Olympics so badly? Other than worldwide recognition, what are the benefits of being an Olympic host city?

10   9   **8**   7   6

Cha-Ching!

Check out this list of facts. These are just some of the dollar amounts of the bribes accepted by six members of the IOC.

$270,000

The value of cash, gifts, and travel and medical expenses accepted by Jean-Claude Ganga of the Republic of Congo

$97,000

The amount of tuition money Lamine Keita of Mali received to pay for his son's university education

$34,650

The amount of cash Charles Mukora received. He claimed he used the money to develop sport activities in Kenya. However, many accused Mukora of using the money for personal use.

$21,000

The value of cash and benefits Ecuador's Agustin Arroyo received

$17,000

The amount of money that was given to the son of expelled Sudanese member Ahmed Abdel Gadir

$10,000

The amount of money donated to Sergio Santander's political campaign in Chile

Take Note

The Salt Lake City scandal takes the #8 spot on our list. It makes us realize that even Olympic officials, who are supposed to maintain fairness, can become involved in shady deals. The scandal resulted in an important change to the IOC. Today, officials cannot accept gifts from bidding cities.

• Find out more about how the International Olympic Committee picks the winning city to host an event. What makes one city more favorable than another?

5 4 3 2 1

7 THE FIXED SC

Jamie Salé and David Pelletier of Canada compete during the 2002 Winter Olympic Games at the Salt Lake Ice Center.

JAMIE SALÉ AND DAVID PELLETIER—GETTY IMAGES

18

ORE

MAJOR PLAYERS: Canadian pairs figure skaters Jamie Salé and David Pelletier; Russian pairs figure skaters Yelena Berezhnaya and Anton Sikharulidze; skating judge Marie-Reine Le Gougne

SHOCK FACTOR: Le Gougne helped award the Russian pair an Olympic gold medal — she later claimed she was pressured to do it.

At the 2002 Winter Olympics, Canadian pairs figure skaters Jamie Salé (Sah-lay) and David Pelletier (Pel-a-tee-ay) were competing against Russian pair Yelena Berezhnaya (Ber-ezh-nie-ah) and Anton Sikharulidze (Sik-ah-ru-leet-zah). Everyone fell in love with Salé and Pelletier's perfect performance. Many figure skating fans were not impressed with the mistakes Berezhnaya and Sikharulidze made in their routine. But the final scores shocked everyone — the gold medal was awarded to the Russian pair!

Shortly after the gold medal was awarded, skating judge Marie-Reine Le Gougne (La Goon-ya) made an outrageous confession: she had fixed her scores so that the Russian pair could win. Read on to see why this scandal is #7 on our list.

THE FIXED SCORE

BEFORE THE STORM

Salé and Pelletier were reigning World Pairs Figure Skating Champions. They had gone into the 2002 Winter Olympics as favorites, but it was clear that they would be in a tight race with the talented Russian team of Berezhnaya and Sikharulidze. According to the Associated Press, Salé and Pelletier's lifts, spins, and jumps were perfect. Surprisingly, in a decision of 5-4, Berezhnaya and Sikharulidze were awarded the gold medal instead of Salé and Pelletier.

A SCANDALOUS AFFAIR

Le Gougne, the French judge, admitted that she was pressured to vote for the Russians as the gold-medal winners. Le Gougne blamed Didier Gailhaguet (Guy-ah-gay), the president of the French Ice Sports Federation, for persuading her to do it. It was also discovered that a member of the Russian mafia, Alimzan Tokhtakhounov (Tot-ah-koo-nauf), was involved in the scam! Investigators tapped into the Russian's phone calls and heard him discuss fixing scores in the Olympics.

THE AFTERMATH

The International Skating Union suspended Le Gougne and Gailhaguet for three years. Tokhtakhounov was charged with bribery and fraud. Salé and Pelletier were awarded gold medals, but Berezhnaya and Sikharulidze were allowed to keep their medals. A new judging system was enforced to prevent cheating. Before the scandal, skating judges gave skaters an automatic perfect score of 6.0. Then the judges would deduct points from the 6.0 score for any mistakes performed. Now, skaters do not get an automatic perfect score; instead, they are only awarded points for the moves they perform.

Besides Le Gougne, the other judges who voted for the Russians were never suspected of cheating. This is because they were from countries that usually voted for Russian competitors.

Quick Fact

ESPN reported that Le Gougne fixed her judging scores as a "vote-swapping deal." She wanted to make sure that French ice dancers Marina Anissina and Gwendal Peizerat also became Olympic champions.

Quick Fact

One of the most famous jumps in figure skating is called an axel. There are single, double, and triple axels. In the Russian pair's Olympic routine, Sikharulidze made a mistake in a double axel.

The Expert Says...

"The ensuing uproar, which resulted in the awarding of gold medals to both teams, cast a pall on the International Skating Union ...

— Richard Corliss, critic and writer for *TIME* magazine

pall: *feeling of gloom*

10   9   8   **7**   6

GOLD FOR SALÉ AND PELLETIER STIRS WORLD REACTION

A report from CBC News
February 16, 2002

Pairs figure skaters Jamie Salé and David Pelletier knew all along they had turned in a solid gold performance at Salt Lake City ... [T]he International Olympic Committee agreed, overturning a controversial judges' decision and awarding the couple a second set of gold medals. ...

Pelletier was equally overjoyed by the decision, and said he had no hard feelings against the Russian pair.

"This was not something against (the Russians)," Pelletier said. "This was against the system ..."

In Moscow on a trade mission, [Canadian] Prime Minister Jean Chrétien said, "I'm happy, congratulations to both of them, and hallelujah."

Even Washington added its two cents worth. U.S. President George W. Bush welcomed the decision to award the second set of golds, calling it the right thing to do. ...

The news wasn't received everywhere with unqualified support though. At her home in Edmonton, [Alberta, Canada,] the pair's home base, Salé's mother, Pattie Siegel, said she was happy, but not overjoyed by the decision. Siegel said she was disturbed that her daughter had been denied the celebration that would have come with an untainted win. ...

This is not the first time that the IOC has altered medal standings. In 1993, Canadian synchronized swimmer Sylvie Frechette's silver medal was replaced with a gold after the IOC ruled a judge's error had deprived her of first place at the [1992] Barcelona Olympics.

untainted: *clean*

Do you think awarding Salé and Pelletier gold medals was enough compensation for the Olympic judging error? Explain your opinion.

Pelletier and Salé remain friends with Berezhnaya and Sikharulidze.

Do you think Salé and Pelletier should have hard feelings against their skating rivals? Explain your answer.

Take Note

At #7, this scandal has made it onto our list because it had a great impact on a sport. It resulted in measures to stop bribery and cheating. Also, a new scoring system was introduced.
• Research this scandal further. How has it affected the careers of the skaters involved?

5 4 3 2 1

In 2003, something fishy was discovered in the Bay Area Laboratory Co-operative (BALCO) in Burlingame, California.

BUST

MAJOR PLAYERS: A sports healthcare clinic and its famous athletic clients

SHOCK FACTOR: This famous nutrition center provided athletes with illegal steroids.

A nutrition center called the Bay Area Laboratory Co-operative (BALCO) had been helping athletes stay healthy since 1984. It had a reputation for providing legal zinc and magnesium supplements, which help boost testosterone levels in athletes. But in 2003, a secret was discovered about the clinic. BALCO founder Victor Conte was providing anabolic steroids to athletes. Anabolic steroids make athletes stronger by enhancing the growth of muscle tissues. But there are side effects to the drugs. Heart damage can occur, which frequently leads to heart attacks. Sometimes male and female users experience deepened voices and baldness. Without the proper prescription, anabolic steroids are illegal to use. These drugs are banned by most major sports associations, including the International Olympic Committee (IOC), the NBA, and the NFL.

The BALCO scandal shattered the careers of many athletes. It also encouraged sport leagues, such as Major League Baseball, to promote healthy lifestyles.

---

testosterone: *hormone important in the development of muscle mass*

THE BALCO BUST

BEFORE THE STORM

BALCO was a nutrition clinic for Olympic athletes and athletes in team sports. The company took urine and blood samples from athletes and tested them for vitamin and mineral deficiencies. After analyzing the samples, BALCO would prescribe nutritional supplements for these sports superstars.

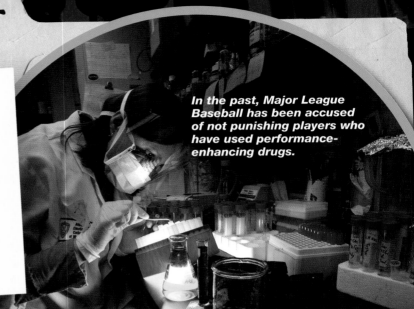

In the past, Major League Baseball has been accused of not punishing players who have used performance-enhancing drugs.

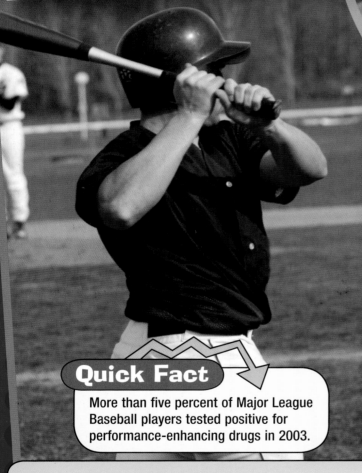

A SCANDALOUS AFFAIR

In June 2003, a track-and-field coach named Trevor Graham contacted the United States Anti-Doping Agency (USADA). He gave the USADA a list of athletes who used anabolic steroids provided by BALCO. The coach also sent the USADA a used needle with evidence of the drug.

THE AFTERMATH

Victor Conte, along with other trainers and clinic executives involved in the scandal, pleaded guilty for distributing illegal steroids. A large number of athletic superstars tested positive for anabolic steroids. They received fines, bans, and penalties. Many sports federations created new drug policies. For example, in 2005, Major League Baseball warned baseball players that they would be randomly tested for drugs.

Quick Fact

More than five percent of Major League Baseball players tested positive for performance-enhancing drugs in 2003.

The Expert Says...

" In the wake of the BALCO scandal, you had a high level of public consciousness and attention to the issue of anabolic steroids in sports. "

— Rick Collins, lawyer and former competitive bodybuilder

consciousness: *awareness*

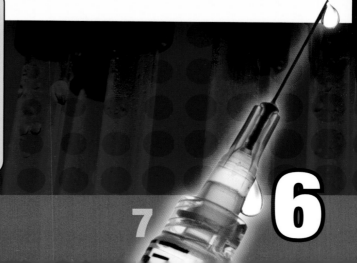

10   **9**   **8**   **7**   **6**

Facing the Consequences

Brian Frasure

Take a look at these profiles of athletes who faced punishments after being caught with anabolic steroids.

Brian Frasure

This amputee track runner tested positive for anabolic steroids at the 2000 Paralympic Games. Frasure's silver medal was taken away. He was also banned from competing in any sports for the next four years, including the 2004 Paralympic Games.

Tim Montgomery

This sprinter faced bans from both relay racing and individual events. His 2001 world record in a 100-meter event and his gold medal from a 2001 World Championship relay race were stripped from him. Montgomery also lost his world record of 9.78 seconds in a 2002 100-meter event.

Chris Cooper, Barret Robbins, and Dana Stubblefield

In the summer of 2004, these football players were punished with heavy fines. They were warned that if they were caught with performance-enhancing drugs again, they would be banned from playing eight games for the year.

Side Effects

Besides heart attacks and baldness, there are other consequences to anabolic steroids. Check out this list of the shocking side effects of steroids.

- Mood swings, aggression, and depression
- Hallucinations and paranoia
- Nausea and vomiting
- Sleeping problems, including frequent fatigue
- High blood pressure
- Puffy feet and legs
- Skin diseases
- Constant breath and body odors

? Find out what happens to an adolescent's height when he or she takes anabolic steroids.

Take Note

The BALCO scandal comes in at #6. It had a major impact on the careers of several famous athletes. Also, it encouraged sports federations to crack down on the use of banned substances.
- Does the controversy surrounding athletes using performance-enhancing drugs affect the way you look at sports and sports heroes? Explain.

4   3   2   1

Although he tried to deny it, Juventus's general manager Luciano Moggi was at the center of the league's match-fixing scandal.

SCANDAL

SHOCK FACTOR: Moggi fixed soccer games, including player and referee selections.

Juventus is one of the most popular soccer teams in the world. In Italy alone, the team has about 10 million fans! Juventus has won many awards, including nine Italian Cups and four Italian Supercups. When a scandal involving the team hit the news in 2006, Italian fans were shocked.

Juventus won its 29th league title in 2006. Shortly after the team celebrated, the media released breaking news: Juventus manager Luciano Moggi had created a powerful match-fixing system. He had spoken to the Italian Football Federation about planning the outcomes of games. Moggi had discussed matching certain referees to games. He had even planned which soccer players should be yellow carded! In soccer, a yellow card is used by the referee to warn a player or coach of misconduct. When players receive two yellow cards, which equal a red card, they are removed from the game.

This match-fixing scandal is shocking because a soccer team's own coach was involved. What's even more shocking about this scandal is how he was busted in the act!

THE SOCCER SCANDAL

BEFORE THE STORM

In 1994, Luciano Moggi became the general manager of Juventus. Rival soccer teams claimed that Moggi was too friendly with referees at soccer games. But everyone assumed these rumors were spread because of jealousy. Juventus was very successful under Moggi. The team won many games, including the European Cup in 1996.

A SCANDALOUS AFFAIR

Newspapers published transcripts of telephone conversations between Moggi and senior officials from the Italian Football Federation. The conversations were about fixing referee appointments and player selections. Later, it was discovered that Moggi even fixed a soccer TV show. He manipulated the show's content, including the criticism of players and games, and poll results from TV viewers!

THE AFTERMATH

When it was revealed that Moggi was pressuring officials, he was suspended from soccer for five years. Since the Italian Football Federation was aware of fixed games, many board members resigned. The Juventus team was forced to drop down a level from Serie A to Serie B, as well as give up their last two Serie A championship titles. After the scandal died down, the attendance at Serie A games decreased. Because Juventus moved to Serie B, the smaller league gained more fans. In 2007, Juventus returned to the Serie A league.

? Think of another sports scandal. How has that controversy affected the fan base?

Quick Fact

The Italian Football Federation has three levels of professional soccer: Serie A, Serie B, and Serie C. Serie A is the top competitive level. Serie B is a less prestigious soccer league.

The Juventus players celebrate a 2006 win.

The Expert Says...

" This has been described as the tsunami of Italian [soccer] … The scandal is so serious that the magistrates investigating it are the ones who usually investigate mafia. "

— Alessio Vinci, anchor and reporter for CNN

magistrates: *public officials with power to administer and enforce laws*

? Do you think it was fair for the whole Juventus team to be punished for Moggi's dishonesty? Explain.

SCANDAL
HITS ITALIAN LEAGUE

A newspaper article from *The Boston Globe*
By Frank Dell'Apa, *Globe* staff
May 23, 2006

... **F**inally, thanks to an enterprising investigative team, one of the biggest corruption scandals in soccer history has been uncovered.

By tapping into telephone conversations, mostly involving Juventus general manager Luciano Moggi, details were revealed as to how Moggi had influenced referee selections, player transfers, candidates for the Italian national team, and even the presentation of a popular television highlights program.

Moggi and the entire board of directors of Juventus resigned, as did the president of Federazione Italiana Gioco Calcio, the game's ruling body, plus the head of the referees' committee, and talk-show host Aldo Biscardi.

Massimo De Santis, Italy's top referee, has been withdrawn from the World Cup list. ...

Moggi ... manipulated the results of key games through blackmail and bribes to referees and also attempted to influence the selection of players represented by Gea World, which is run by his son, Alessandro Moggi. Gea represents 262 players, 31 club officials, and 29 coaches in Italy.

enterprising: *creative*
player transfers: *moving players from one team to another*

Former Juventus player Gianluca Zambrotta dribbles the ball.

Quick Fact

In the 2005/2006 season, it was discovered that other Serie A soccer officials were fixing games. Officials were from the teams Reggina, A.C. Milan, Lazio, and Fiorentina. All of these teams had points taken away from the upcoming soccer season.

Take Note

This soccer scandal has deservedly landed a spot at #5. It tarnished the reputation of a team with a 110-year history of soccer excellence. This scandal rocked the world of soccer and even had an effect on attendance at games.
- Compare what Moggi did to providing performance-enhancing drugs to athletes, or placing bets on or against a team. Were Moggi's actions worse? Why?

5   4   3   2   1

4 HARDING VS.

Tonya Harding (right) and Nancy Kerrigan share a tense moment on the ice. This photo was taken less than a month after Harding's ex-husband attacked Kerrigan, hoping to improve Harding's chances at the Olympics.

TONYA HARDING AND NANCY KERRIGAN–AFP/GETTY IMAGES

KERRIGAN

MAJOR PLAYERS: Figure skaters Tonya Harding and Nancy Kerrigan

SHOCK FACTOR: Harding was involved in a wicked scheme to injure her figure-skating rival.

In 1991, figure skater Tonya Harding accomplished an amazing feat. She became the first American woman to complete a triple axel during a competition! But three years later, Harding would face a career turnaround.

Harding might have made skating history with her triple axel, but Kerrigan was known as the best female figure skater in the U.S. She was dubbed "America's ice queen." On the afternoon of January 6, 1994, Nancy Kerrigan was hit in the knee by an attacker. She couldn't compete in the United States Figure Skating Championships because of her knee injury. This competition was very important. It determined who would compete at the 1994 Winter Olympics.

Shortly after the attack, the plan to hurt Kerrigan was revealed. It was the scheme of Harding's bodyguard and her ex-husband. They wanted to increase Harding's chances of making it to the Olympics. Harding denied having a part in the scheme, but soon the truth was revealed.

BEFORE THE STORM

On the fateful day, Kerrigan had stopped to talk to a reporter after a training session. Suddenly, a young man pulled out a metal baton and struck Kerrigan above her right kneecap! Kerrigan fell to the ground. As she was screaming in pain, the attacker ran away. Because of the injury, Kerrigan had to withdraw from the Championships. Tonya Harding, her chief rival, won the Championships and a spot on the U.S. Olympic skating team.

Quick Fact

The U.S. figure skating officials recognized that Kerrigan could not compete for the Championships because of the assault. They made a decision to let her compete at the Olympics in Lillehammer, Norway, in 1994.

A SCANDALOUS AFFAIR

In an interview with the FBI, Jeff Gillooly (Harding's ex-husband) revealed that Harding had approved the plan to injure Kerrigan. Harding took it upon herself to find out where Kerrigan was practicing on the day of the attack. When Harding was confronted by investigators, she claimed that she had no role in the assault. But Harding ended up pleading guilty for lying about her connection to the crime. She had to pay fines and perform community service. Gillooly was fined $100,000, and sentenced to two years in prison. His accomplices in the scheme were put behind bars for 18 months.

A doctor examines Nancy Kerrigan's knees after the brutal attack.

THE AFTERMATH

After Kerrigan had healed and the Olympics began, there was a media-hyped showdown between Harding and Kerrigan. But neither came away with the gold medal. It went to Ukrainian skater Oksana Baiul. Kerrigan won a silver medal, which led to product endorsements.

---

endorsements: *acts where someone is a spokesperson for a product or service*

In the 1994 Winter Olympics, Harding had a skate lace problem that resulted in her tearful plea to have it fixed. The judges allowed her a restart.

Quick Fact

The U.S. Figure Skating Association banned Harding from skating for life, and also from becoming a skating coach!

Harding Headlines

The media was obsessed with this figure-skating scandal. Check out these press clippings for a few examples of how the scandal was reported.

SHE CAN SKATE BUT SHE CAN'T HIDE

Newsweek, February 7, 1994

… Harding's ex-husband is said to have told FBI agents that Harding took part in planning the attack and subsequent cover-up of her involvement.

subsequent: *later*

HARDING STRIPPED OF TITLE; BANNED FOR LIFE

The Washington Post, July 1, 1994

… the U.S. Figure Skating Association yesterday stripped Tonya Harding of her 1994 national championship and banned her from the organization for life.

 How do you think favorable and unfavorable media attention can affect an athlete's career?

HARDING BIDS ADIEU SKATING TO LOVE SONG

The New York Times, February 15, 1994

Tonya Harding bid her loyal supporters goodbye today after a final public practice before the Olympics. …

Harding's sentence affirmed

St. Petersburg Times, August 31, 1995

… As part of the plea bargain, Harding is to donate $50,000 to Special Olympics and perform 500 hours of community service.

The Expert Says …

 Skating was big … But this incident … was heard around the world.

— Tom Collins, creator of the *Champions on Ice* tour

Take Note

At #4, the Tonya Harding–Nancy Kerrigan scandal grabbed headlines around the world, affected the careers of two talented figure skaters, and affected the popularity of figure skating as a sport.
- Why do you think people around the world were so fascinated by this scandal? Explain your reason.

5   **4**   3   2   1

THE GAMBLING

Allegations of gambling turned this former baseball manager's life upside down.

NO-NO

MAJOR PLAYER: Cincinnati Reds manager Pete Rose

SHOCK FACTOR: In the early months of 1989, it became clear that Pete Rose was betting large sums of money on baseball — a major no-no.

Baseball fans admired Pete Rose for his outstanding achievements. Rose had 4,256 base hits in his career, a major league record. He also holds the records for games played, and was chosen to play in the All-Star Game an amazing 17 times. In 1975, Rose was honored as the World Series Most Valuable Player. Nicknamed "Charlie Hustle," Rose was also famous for his head-first slides and for sprinting to first base after being walked.

But Rose shocked the world of baseball in the late 1980s. While he was managing the Cincinnati Reds, the Major League Baseball learned that he was gambling money on baseball games (Rose would bet at least $1,000 per game). This is definitely against the rules. Major League Baseball has some serious regulations, including Rule 21(d). It states that any member of the Major League who gambles on baseball will face suspension. If any of these members gambles on a game involving his team, then that person will be kicked out of the league.

Despite his success as an athlete and manager, Rose did not get away with his wrongdoing. In fact, it ended his baseball career.

BEFORE THE STORM

Rose was already a baseball player for the Cincinnati Reds when he became the manager of the team in 1984. Rose helped the Cincinnati Reds become successful in the mid-1980s. While Rose was the team's coach, the Reds finished in second place four consecutive times.

A SCANDALOUS AFFAIR

Rumors flew about Rose gambling on baseball games. The rumors also claimed that he bet against his own team! Major League officials commissioned a lawyer, John Dowd, to investigate Rose. Dowd could not prove that Rose gambled against the Reds. However, Dowd discovered that Rose bet on 52 games in 1987.

THE AFTERMATH

Even though Rose denied gambling on baseball, he accepted a lifetime ban from Major League Baseball. In his 2004 autobiography, he finally admitted to gambling. Rose claimed that he bet on the Cincinnati Reds, "but never to lose." Rose is not allowed to be a member of the National Baseball Hall of Fame. He asked the Hall to review his status in 1997. As of 2007, the Hall has continued to reject Rose.

commissioned: *hired*

? If you were a player, why wouldn't you want your manager betting against your own team? Explain.

Quick Fact

In August 1989, Rose was fired as the Reds' manager. He was replaced by Tommy Helms.

Quick Fact

Rose had a reputation for being a very competitive baseball player. At the 1970 All-Star Game, Rose slammed into Cleveland Indians catcher Ray Fosse to get to home plate. As a result of the collision, Fosse suffered a serious shoulder injury, which forced him into early retirement.

The Expert Says...

" Rose has been able to assume some responsibility for his gambling problems, but it is not apparent that he has been completely honest with himself and the public. "

— Ron Briley, teacher and writer for George Mason University's History News Network Web site

apparent: *obvious*

THE LIFE OF A ROSE

This timeline describes a few of Rose's athletic and non-athletic actions that made media headlines.

May 1988: Rose is suspended for 30 days for shoving umpire Dave Pallone.

April 1990: Caught cheating! Rose is guilty of not reporting all his income on tax returns. Rose was punished with five months in prison, a fine of $5,000, and 1,000 hours of community service in schools.

August 1990: Rose begins his prison sentence for cheating on his income tax. The prison puts Rose to work in a machine shop, where he earns 11 cents per day.

March 1998: Rose makes an appearance on *WrestleMania XIV*. The world watches him wrestle with Kane, a famous World Wrestling Entertainment (WWE) wrestler.

November 1999: Via the World Wide Web, Rose starts a petition for fans to request his membership in the National Baseball Hall of Fame.

January 2004: Rose openly admits he has gambled on baseball in his autobiography, *Pete Rose: My Prison Without Bars*. After its release, it is #1 on the *New York Times* list of nonfiction hardcover best sellers.

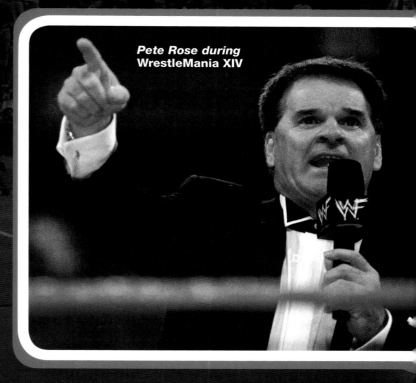

Pete Rose during WrestleMania XIV

Quick Fact

In 2004, Rose was inducted into the WWE Hall of Fame for appearing in *WrestleMania*.

 Do you agree with Pete Rose's punishment for gambling? Explain your reason.

Take Note

This scandal slides into the #3 spot on our list because it shows us just how far our heroes can fall. Rose had to deal with intense shame and some pretty severe consequences.

• If Rose is considered an accomplished baseball player, do you think he should be in the Hall of Fame? Should players be judged on their behavior or how well they play? Explain.

5　　　4　　　**3**　　　2　　　1

This victory didn't last long! Ben Johnson (pointing) was stripped of his gold medal after testing positive for steroids at the 1988 Summer Olympics in Seoul, South Korea.

BEN JOHNSON'S WIN—© GILBERT IUNDT, JEAN-YVES RUSZNIEWSKI/TEMPSPORT/CORBIS

TAKE

MAJOR PLAYER: Canadian track star Ben Johnson

SHOCK FACTOR: Urine tests revealed that Johnson was taking performance-enhancing drugs.

Imagine taking just 48 running steps to win an Olympic gold medal. That's exactly what Ben Johnson did at the 1988 Summer Olympics in Seoul, South Korea!

Johnson ran at a speed of 30 mph. He won a gold medal in the 100-meter dash. Earning a silver medal in the same race was Johnson's rival Carl Lewis. Johnson's life changed 62 hours after the race. The whole world learned about his secret: he was using anabolic steroids.

The scandal disappointed Johnson's track and field fans. It also stunned the International Olympic Committee (IOC). The IOC took back Johnson's gold medal. However, this was only part of Johnson's punishment. Check out the consequences of Johnson's action, and see how this scandal made a permanent mark in sports.

JOHNSON'S MISTAKE

BEFORE THE STORM

Ben Johnson won an Olympic gold medal and set a new world record when he completed the 100-meter dash in 9.79 seconds. Johnson became known — briefly — as the world's fastest man.

A SCANDALOUS AFFAIR

Johnson's urine was tested immediately after he won the 100-meter race. He tested positive for anabolic steroids. At first, Johnson told the IOC that someone must have drugged his herbal drink before the race. But then Johnson admitted to using steroids. His coach also came forward and revealed that Johnson had used anabolic steroids, plus other performance-enhancing drugs, since 1981.

THE AFTERMATH

The 1988 gold medal went to Carl Lewis instead. Johnson's gold medal and world records were stripped from him. Johnson also faced a two-year ban from competing in tournaments. Because of the scandal, the Canadian government investigated drug abuse in sports. In 1991, a Canadian drug-testing program began, which helped to encourage athletes to train in a healthy manner.

Ben Johnson breaks from the pack during the 100-meter race of the 1988 Summer Olympic Games in Seoul.

10   9   8   7   6

A LESSON LEARNED

These quotes highlight how the media responded to Ben Johnson's use of steroids.

Ben Johnson, 2007

"[Ben Johnson] brought the steroid debate front and center and into the court of public opinion."
— Stan Grossfeld, *The Boston Globe*

"Ben Johnson has not only rained on their parade ... he's absolutely flooded it."
— Brian Williams, CBC anchorman, referring to the disappointment of the Olympics' South Korean organizers

"Spectators felt deceived and non-using athletes felt [cheated]."
— Daniel Benjamin, *TIME* magazine

Johnson failed another drug test in 1993. This was inexcusable to the International Amateur Athletics Federation (IAAF). The IAFF punished Johnson with a ban from track and field events for life.

The Canadian sprinter has realized that his mistakes have had an impact on his life. In a discussion with the *Yale Herald*, he was not afraid to admit that he learned a lesson. According to Johnson: "I want to help in any way I can to ensure that kids and athletes are aware and know not to take drugs."

? What do you think Johnson should do to inform athletes about the dangers of drugs?

The Expert Says...

" [The scandal] spelt utter disaster for Canada and the Canadians back home who had celebrated ... the gold-winning feat. "

— K.N. Anand, writer for *The Hindu*

Take Note

The Ben Johnson scandal is #2 on our list. It ruined the career of an Olympic athlete. It also made sports fans and the media realize that steroids are commonly used in professional sports. As a result, drug testing has improved and become more frequent in sports.
• How would you feel if someone you knew cheated in sports or on a test? Explain your answer.

2

5   4   3   1

Hundreds of baseball fans sat in the courtroom to hear the Black Sox verdict. When they were found not guilty, the spectators shouted, "Hooray for the clean Sox!"

FUL SOX

WHITESOX–© BETTMANN/CORBIS

MAJOR PLAYERS: Eight members of the Chicago White Sox

SHOCK FACTOR: Baseball players intentionally lost the World Series!

It's a shame when an athlete is banned from a sport. But it's a bigger bombshell when eight teammates are banned at the same time!

In 1919, the Chicago White Sox were very successful in the world of baseball. But the players were unhappy because of their low salaries. Greed finally got the better of these players from the Chicago White Sox and they became involved in a gambling scandal. White Sox first baseman Chick Gandil approached seven teammates with a plan that would earn them thousands of dollars — they would rig the World Series. Gandil approached pitchers Eddie Cicotte and Claude Williams, left-fielder "Shoeless" Joe Jackson, third baseman Buck Weaver; shortstop Swede Risberg, centerfielder Oscar Felsch, and infielder Fred McMullin. Together, these eight players fixed the 1919 World Series so that the White Sox would lose to the Cincinnati Reds.

These guilty players, who were nicknamed the "Black Sox," faced major consequences that included a lifetime ban from baseball. According to the *Chicago Tribune*, their punishment helped put a stop to shady behavior such as gambling in baseball. Professional baseball did not face another gambling scandal until 1989, when Pete Rose was banned from the sport.

 Do you think cheating in a baseball game for the purpose of betting is easily done? Explain.

THE SHAMEFUL SOX

BEFORE THE STORM

The Cincinnati Reds and the Chicago White Sox were considered the best baseball teams of 1919. Baseball reporters and fans believed that the Reds would lose to the White Sox. The Sox's pitcher, Eddie Cicotte, had 29 wins and only seven losses. He was considered better than the Reds' top pitchers. At the end of the 1919 World Series, the Sox lost to the Cincinnati Reds.

A SCANDALOUS AFFAIR

In 1920, a grand jury was investigating a fixed game between the Chicago Cubs and the Philadelphia Phillies. But this led to an investigation into the 1919 World Series. It turned out that Gandil was the mastermind who approached gamblers about fixing the World Series. The players were offered $10,000 in advance, plus payments of $70,000 over the first four World Series games.

Eddie Cicotte

Quick Fact

Eddie Cicotte was making $6,000 a year as a Chicago White Sox pitcher. Now the average salary of a Chicago White Sox player is over $2,000,000!

THE AFTERMATH

The players were put on trial for fixing the World Series. The jury did not find them guilty. Also, somebody stole the players' written confessions, so these could not be used as evidence against the players. As punishment, the commissioner of baseball banned the Black Sox from the sport anyway. Plus, the players were denied entry into the National Baseball Hall of Fame. The scandal became the subject of many books and movies, including the film *Eight Men Out*.

"SHOELESS" JOE JACKSON

The Expert Says...

" Covering the White Sox who had become Black Sox became a full-time vocation for some sports and court reporters in the U.S. "

— George Grace, sports columnist for *The Sudbury Star*

vocation: *job*

Why do you think the expert said the Black Sox scandal was a "full-time vocation" for reporters?

EDDIE CICOTTE, JOE JACKSON—LOC; JOHN CUSACK—PHOTO BY ORION PICTURES/KPA-ZUMA/KEYSTONE PRESS; ALL OTHER IMAGES–SHUTTERSTOCK.ISTOCKPHOTO

8   7   6

DIRECTOR JOHN SAYLES TAKES HIS RUN AT PLATE

By Bruce Blackadar
A movie review from the *Toronto Star*
August 31, 1988

Eight Men Out … is about the notorious 1919 World Series scandal involving the Chicago White Sox players who were seduced by slick gamblers into throwing games against the Cincinnati Reds. …

Director/writer John Sayles … wanted to make a movie about the scandal … for more than a decade. …

[John] Cusack plays Buck Weaver, the hapless third baseman, who, although he didn't take any money and played errorless ball while his teammates were fixing the series, was banished nonetheless from the game he adored.

Right until he died in 1956, Weaver desperately tried to clear his name. Cusack … says he ended up having sympathy with "the whole ball club" while he was making the movie. …

The players then had no pension, they had an owner who was greedy and uncaring, and Cusack sees an analogy between the athletes and actors.

"We are used by others to make money, and I understand their (the ballplayers) frustration. They use your spirit and energy and package, and then when you see it, it's something else."

Of the real "Shoeless Joe" [actor D.B.] Sweeney says: "He had the worst luck. If he'd played 15 years later than he did he would have been considered the greatest player ever. His accomplishments as a ballplayer have been buried."

---

notorious: *famous for an unfavorable act*
hapless: *unlucky*
analogy: *comparison*

Actor John Cusack as Buck Weaver in Eight Men Out

Quick Fact

Many sports fans believed that the Black Sox scandal resulted in a curse. The Chicago White Sox did not win another World Series until 2005. In 1959, the team won games one and five of the World Series.

Take Note

The scandal involving the "eight men out" comes in at #1 on our list. It was the ultimate betrayal of a national pastime and its adoring fans. There is no bigger sports scandal than this one!
• The Chicago White Sox scandal has been the subject of popular books and films. Why do you think it has captured the public's imagination?

5   4   3   2   1

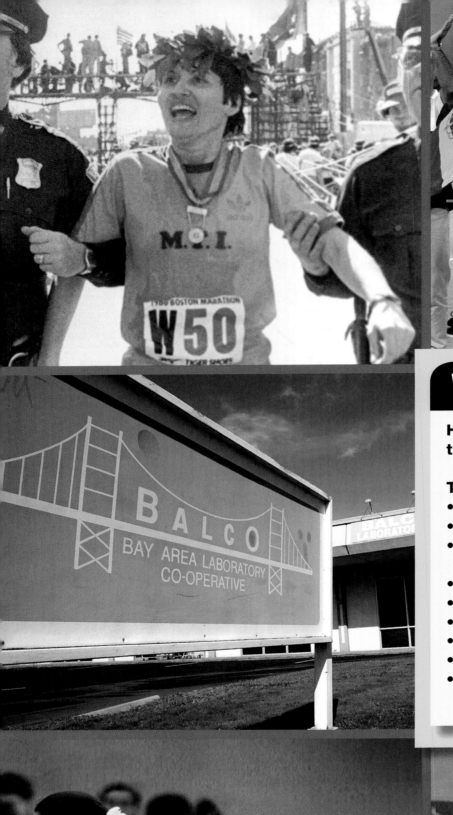

We Thought ...

Here are the criteria we used in ranking the 10 most shocking sports scandals.

The scandal:
- Attracted a great deal of media attention
- Caused the rules to be changed in a sport
- Brought great shame and embarrassment to athletes, teams, and nations
- Involved corrupt officials
- Affected the careers of the athletes involved
- Caused athletes and teams to lose gold medals
- Brought about new judging systems
- Captured the imagination of the public
- Resulted in severe consequences

What Do You Think?

1. Do you agree with our ranking? If you don't, try ranking them yourself. Justify your ranking with data from your own research and reasoning. You may refer to our criteria, or you may want to draw up your own list of criteria.

2. Here are three other sports scandals we considered but in the end did not include in our top 10 list: Little League baseball pitcher Danny Almonte lying about his age; Wayne Gretzky's betting scandal; and Sammy Sosa's corked baseball bat.
   - Find out more about these scandals. Do you think they should have made our list? Give reasons for your response.
   - Are there other sports scandals that you think should have made our list? Explain your choices.

Index